The Tao of Leadership

The Tao of Leadership

Lao Tzu's *Tao Te Ching*
Adapted for a New Age

John Heider

HUMANICS NEW AGE
Atlanta, Georgia

Humanics New Age
P.O.Box 7400
Atlanta, Georgia 30309

Humanics New Age is an imprint of Humanics Limited

Sixth Printing -Revised 1994

Many illustrations are from *The Mustard Seed Garden Manual of Painting*,
translated from the Chinese and edited by Mai-mai Sze, Bollingen Series,
Princeton University Press, New York, 1956. These illustrations, originally
reproduced by wood block printing, were created in the seventeenth century
by three brothers: Wang Kei, Wang Shih, and Wang Nieh.

PRINTED IN THE UNITED STATES OF AMERICA

Library of Congress Cataloging in Publication Data
Heider, John.
              The Tao of Leadership

              1. Lao-tzu.   Tao te ching   2. Leadership   I. Lao-tzu.
Tao te ching.   II. Title
BL1900. L35H49   1984   299'. 51482   84-19750
ISBN 0-89334-079-0

Dedicated to the faculty, staff, students, and
friends of The Human Potential School of Mendocino

Author's Note

Nearly all versions of *Tao Te Ching,* including the six listed in the Bibliography, use the same system of numbering chapters that I have used here. This makes comparisons between different versions easy.

Acknowledgments

My deepest thanks go to the many readers, auditors, and editors whose comments and corrections have brought this book to its final form.

Special thanks to Tom Conn for introducing *The Tao of Leadership* to Gary Wilson of Humanics Limited.

The Titles of the Chapters

Introduction

Lao Tzu's *Tao Te Ching* is one of China's best loved books of wisdom. It was originally addressed to the sage and to the wise political ruler of the fifth century B.C. It comes down to us as a classic of world literature, and many of Lao Tzu's sayings will be familiar to you. For example: "The journey of a thousand miles begins with a single step."

As a teacher, I have found the *Tao Te Ching* an indispensable text in workshops for group leaders, psychotherapists, and humanistic educators. Students like it. It is simple and it makes sense. But even more important is the fact that *Tao Te Ching* persuasively unites leadership skills and the leader's way of life: *our work is our path.*

My success with using *Tao* led me to see its broader applicability, especially to a new generation so fascinated with the role of the leader and the skillful management of human resources. This adaptation, I believe, will be of value to anyone who aspires to a leadership position, whether within the family or group, church or school, business or military, politics or governmental administration.

Tao Te Ching means the Book (*Ching*) of How (*Tao*) Things Happen or Work (*Te*). The title is pronounced Dow Duh Jing— Dow is like "down" without the "n"; Duh is like the "du" in "duck"; and "jing" rhymes with "ring" or "sing"—and the book itself has three topics:

1. Natural law, or how things happen;

2. A way of life, or how to live in conscious harmony with natural law;

3. A method of leadership, or how to govern or educate others in accordance with natural law.

Lao Tzu's work, as I have noted, was originally directed to the wise political and governmental leaders of ancient China. I do not read Chinese, however; I made this adaptation by comparing many different translations until their apparent contradictions were reconciled and made sense to me. Then I read one or another translation to my students. Afterward I told them what each passage meant to me and how it applies specifically to a group leader and generally to any individual searching for the personal fulfillment of life's potentialities.

This adaptation of the *Tao* comes from those classes; it is my own version of the meaning of Lao Tzu's own words. Sometimes when the traditional English version is especially beautiful or familiar, however, I have made no changes. In chapter 64, for example, I did not have the heart to alter the classic line noted above.

Thus this version of the *Tao* took form in spoken language. The words, I think, become clearer when read aloud. Try it. Reading aloud is a wholesome custom.

John Heider

Coconut Grove, Florida

The Tao of Leadership

1. Tao Means How

Tao means how: how things happen, how things work. Tao is the single principle underlying all creation. Tao is God.

Tao cannot be defined, because it applies to everything. You cannot define something in terms of itself.

If you can define a principle, it is not Tao.

Tao is a principle. Creation, on the other hand, is a process. That is all there is: principle and process, how and what.

All creation unfolds according to Tao. There is no other way.

Tao cannot be defined, but Tao can be known. The method is meditation, or being aware of what is happening. By being aware of what is happening, I begin to sense how it is happening. I begin to sense Tao.

To become aware of what is happening, I must pay attention with an open mind. I must set aside my personal prejudices or bias. Prejudiced people see only what fits those prejudices.

The method of meditation works, because principle and process are inseparable. All process reveals the underlying principle. This means that I can know Tao. I can know God.

By knowing Tao, I know how things happen.

2. Polarities

All behavior consists of opposites or polarities. If I do anything more and more, over and over, its polarity will appear.

For example, striving to be beautiful makes a person ugly, and trying too hard to be kind is a form of selfishness.

Any over-determined behavior produces its opposite:

- An obsession with living suggests worry about dying.
- True simplicity is not easy.
- Is it a long time or a short time since we last met?
- The braggart probably feels small and insecure.
- Who would be first ends up last.

Knowing how polarities work, the wise leader does not push to make things happen, but allows process to unfold on its own.

The leader teaches by example rather than by lecturing others on how they ought to be.

The leader knows that constant interventions will block the group's process. The leader does not insist that things come out a certain way.

The wise leader does not seek a lot of money or a lot of praise. Nevertheless, there is plenty of both.

3. Being Oneself

The wise leader does not make a show of holiness or pass out grades for good performance. That would create a climate of success and failure. Competition and jealousy follow.

Emphasizing material success is the same: those who have a lot become greedy, and those who have little become thieves.

When you reinforce appearances, people scramble to please.

The wise leader pays respectful attention to all behavior. Thus the group becomes open to more and more possibilities of behavior. People learn a great deal when they are open to everything and not just figuring out what pleases the teacher.

The leader shows that style is no substitute for substance, that knowing certain facts is not more powerful than simple wisdom, that creating an impression is not more potent than acting from one's center.

The students learn that effective action arises out of silence and a clear sense of being. In this they find a source of peace. They discover that the person who is down-to-earth can do what needs doing more effectively than the person who is merely busy.

4. Tao Is Not a Thing

Dig as deep as you will, you will never come to a thing called Tao or God. Tao is not a thing. Tao is a principle or law. Tao means how.

All things behave according to Tao, but Tao does not behave. Tao is never an object or a process.

Tao is the law of all things, of all events. Tao is the common ground of all creation.

Creation consists of things and events. All things and events are vibratory. Vibration consists of opposites or polarities. Polarities may cooperate with one another, or they may conflict to varying degrees.

All things and events, whether they are cooperative or conflicting, harmonious or turbulent, take their form and become resolved in accordance with Tao.

But Tao is not a vibratory event. Tao is not, for example, a sound. Tao has no opposites or polarities. Tao is one; Tao is unity.

As far as I know, nothing comes before Tao. Nothing made Tao. Nothing created God.

5. Equal Treatment

Natural law is blind, its justice evenhanded. The consequences of one's behavior are inescapable. Being human is no excuse.

The wise leader does not try to protect people from themselves. The light of awareness shines equally on what is pleasant and on what is not pleasant.

People are not better than the rest of creation. The same principle which underlies human beings underlies everything equally.

Neither is one person or one people better than the rest of humanity. The same principle is everywhere. One person is as worthy as the next. Why play favorites?

Everything demonstrates the law. Just because God is not a thing does not mean that God is nothing. A little humility is in order.

Knowing this, the leader does not pretend to be special. The leader does not gossip about others or waste breath arguing the merits of competing theories.

Silence is a great source of strength.

6. The Pond in the Valley

Can you learn to become open and receptive, quiet and without desires or the need to do something?

Being open and receptive is called *Yin*, the feminine, or the valley.

Imagine that there is a pond in this valley. When no fears or desires stir the surface of the pond, the water forms a perfect mirror.

In this mirror, you can see the reflection of Tao. You can see God and you can see creation.

Go into the valley, be still, and watch the pond. Go as often as you wish. Your silence will grow. The pond will never run dry.

The valley, the pond, and Tao are all within you.

7. Selflessness

True self-interest teaches selflessness.

Heaven and earth endure because they are not simply selfish but exist in behalf of all creation.

The wise leader, knowing this, keeps egocentricity in check and by doing so becomes even more effective.

Enlightened leadership is service, not selfishness. The leader grows more and lasts longer by placing the well-being of all above the well-being of self alone.

Paradox: By being selfless, the leader enhances self.

8. Water

The wise leader is like water.

Consider water: water cleanses and refreshes all creatures without distinction and without judgment; water freely and fearlessly goes deep beneath the surface of things; water is fluid and responsive; water follows the law freely.

Consider the leader: the leader works in any setting without complaint, with any person or issue that comes on the floor; the leader acts so that all will benefit and serves well regardless of the rate of pay; the leader speaks simply and honestly and intervenes in order to shed light and create harmony.

From watching the movements of water, the leader has learned that in action, timing is everything.

Like water, the leader is yielding. Because the leader does not push, the group does not resent or resist.

9. A Good Group

A good group is better than a spectacular group.

When leaders become superstars, the teacher outshines the teaching.

Very few superstars are down-to-earth. Fame breeds fame, and before long they get carried away with themselves. Then they fly off center and crash.

The wise leader settles for good work and then lets others have the floor. The leader does not take all the credit for what happens and has no need for fame.

A moderate ego demonstrates wisdom.

10. Unbiased Leadership

Can you mediate emotional issues without taking sides or picking favorites?

Can you breathe freely and remain relaxed even in the presence of passionate fears and desires?

Are your own conflicts clarified? Is your own house clean?

Can you be gentle with all factions and lead the group without dominating?

Can you remain open and receptive, no matter what issues arise?

Can you know what is emerging, yet keep your peace while others discover for themselves?

Learn to lead in a nourishing manner.

Learn to lead without being possessive.

Learn to be helpful without taking the credit.

Learn to lead without coercion.

You can do this if you remain unbiased, clear, and down-to-earth.

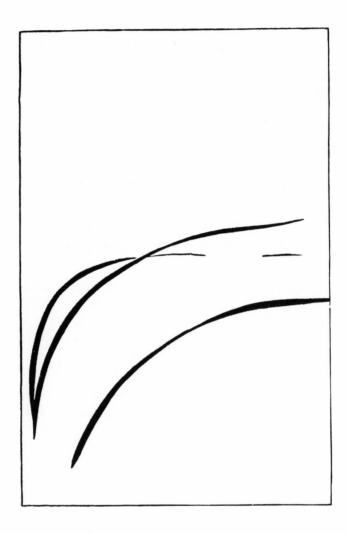

11. The Group Field

Pay attention to silence. What is happening when nothing is happening in a group? That is the group field.

Thirteen people sit in a circle, but it is the climate or the spirit in the center of the circle, where nothing is happening, that determines the nature of the group field.

Learn to see emptiness. When you enter an empty house, can you feel the mood of the place? It is the same with a vase or a pot; learn to see the emptiness inside, which is the usefulness of it.

People's speech and actions are figural events. They give the group form and content.

The silences and empty spaces, on the other hand, reveal the group's essential mood, the context for everything that happens. That is the group field.

12. Time for Reflection

ndless drama in a group clouds consciousness. Too much noise overwhelms the senses. Continual input obscures genuine insight.
Do not substitute sensationalism for learning.

Allow regular time for silent reflection. Turn inward and digest what has happened. Let the senses rest and grow still.

Teach people to let go of their superficial mental chatter and obsessions. Teach people to pay attention to the whole body's reaction to a situation.

When group members have time to reflect, they can see more clearly what is essential in themselves and others.

13. Success

If you measure success in terms of praise and criticism, your anxiety will be endless.

Having a good reputation or becoming well-known for your work can be a hindrance to your further development.

Fame is as burdensome as caring for yourself properly.

What is the problem with praise and criticism?

If the group applauds one thing you do, and then you feel good, you will worry if they do not applaud as loudly the next time. If they are critical, if they argue or complain, you will feel hurt. Either way, you are anxious and dependent.

How can a good reputation be a hindrance?

A good reputation naturally arises from doing good work. But if you try to cherish your reputation, if you try to preserve it, you lose the freedom and honesty necessary for further development.

How is fame like caring for yourself?

In order to do good work, you must take good care of yourself. You must value yourself and allow others to value you also. But if you make too much of yourself, you will become egocentric. Egocentricity injures both self and work.

If you can live with the fruits of success and care for yourself properly, you will be able to foster success in other people.

14. Knowing What Is Happening

When you cannot see what is happening in a group, do not stare harder. Relax and look gently with your inner eye.

When you do not understand what a person is saying, do not grasp for every word. Give up your efforts. Become silent inside and listen with your deepest self.

When you are puzzled by what you see or hear, do not strive to figure things out. Stand back for a moment and become calm. When a person is calm, complex events appear simple.

To know what is happening, push less, open out and be aware. See without staring. Listen quietly rather than listening hard. Use intuition and reflection rather than trying to figure things out.

The more you can let go of trying, and the more open and receptive you become, the more easily you will know what is happening.

Also, stay in the present. The present is more available than either memories of the past or fantasies of the future.

So attend to what is happening now.

15. The Leader's Teachers

They practiced meditation. Meditation made them good at seeing how things happen. Meditation grounded them in the infinite. That is why they sometimes appeared deep and inscrutable, sometimes even great.

Their leadership did not rest on technique or on theatrics, but on silence and on their ability to pay attention.

They moved with grace and awareness, and they were able to negotiate complex situations safely.

They were considerate. They did no injury. They were courteous and quiet, like guests. They knew how to yield gracefully and how to be natural and inconspicuous.

They were as open and receptive and available as the valleys that lie among the hills.

They could clarify events for others, because they had done it for themselves. They could speak to the depths of another person, because they had known their own deeper conflicts and blocks.

Because they had given up selfishness, they could enhance others.

They were not trying to become enlightened, because they were enlightened.

16. Giving Up Selfishness

To become more profound, give up your selfishness. Let go of your efforts to be perfect or rich or secure or admired. Such efforts only limit you. They block your universality.

Letting go is like dying. Everything emerges, becomes formed, and dies. You, too.

When you die, you give up selfishness. You become one with everything else.

My deeper self knows that I am one with everything else anyway. All creation is a single whole which works according to a single principle.

I let my selfishness go and give up the illusion of being separate. I act in behalf of the whole. I benefit me and I benefit you. I am at odds with no one. I am at peace, and have energy to spare, because I am not resisting what is happening.

Death is not frightening, because I know how to let go, and I know the nature of the Eternal.

17. Being a Midwife

The wise leader does not intervene unnecessarily. The leader's presence is felt, but often the group runs itself.

Lesser leaders do a lot, say a lot, have followers, and form cults.

Even worse ones use fear to energize the group and force to overcome resistance.

Only the most dreadful leaders have bad reputations.

Remember that you are facilitating another person's process. It is not your process. Do not intrude. Do not control. Do not force your own needs and insights into the foreground.

If you do not trust a person's process, that person will not trust you.

Imagine that you are a midwife; you are assisting at someone else's birth. Do good without show or fuss. Facilitate what is happening rather than what you think ought to be happening. If you must take the lead, lead so that the mother is helped, yet still free and in charge.

When the baby is born, the mother will rightly say: "We did it ourselves!"

18. This Versus That

Do not lose sight of the single principle: how everything works.

When this principle is lost and the method of meditating on process fails, the group becomes mired in intellectual discussion of what could have happened, what should have happened, what this technique or that might do. Soon the group will be quarrelsome and depressed.

Once you leave the path of simple consciousness, you enter the labyrinth of cleverness, competition, and imitation.

When a person forgets that all creation is a unity, allegiance goes to lesser wholes such as the family, the home team, or the company.

Nationalism, racism, classism, sexism: all arise as consciousness of unity is lost. People take sides and favor this versus that.

19. Self-Improvement

Forget those clever techniques and self-improvement programs, and everyone will be better off.

Do not promise to cure people, to make people feel good, to make life sane or fair or humane. Do not offer programs that appeal to selfishness, programs that teach how to be rich, powerful, sexy — and greedy, paranoid, and manipulative.

No teacher can make you be happy, prosperous, healthy, or powerful. No rules or techniques can enforce these qualities.

If you wish to improve yourself, try silence or some other cleansing discipline that will gradually show you your true selfless self.

20. Traditional Wisdom

Our job is to facilitate process and clarify conflicts. This ability depends less on formal education than on common sense and traditional wisdom.

The highly educated leader tends to respond in terms of one theoretical model or another. It is better simply to respond directly to what is happening here and now.

Make sure that any model you do have is compatible with traditional wisdom: admire the wise of all religions.

For example, most people act in order to fulfill their desires. They believe that the world serves them. But the wise leader serves others and is relatively desireless, even defenseless.

Most people are plagued by endless needs, but the wise leader is content with relatively little. Most people lead busy lives, but the wise leader is quiet and reflective. Most people seek stimulation and novelty, but the wise leader prefers what is common and natural.

Being content permits simplicity in life. What is common is universal. What is natural is close to the source of creation.

This is traditional wisdom.

21. Tao Is Universal

All power and effectiveness come from following the law of creation. There is no substitute for knowing how things happen and for acting accordingly.

Everything, like it or not, is bound by this principle. The principle is like the blueprint for everything.

All power derives from conscious or unconscious cooperation with the principle.

The single principle is manifest everywhere, all the time.

All birth and growth and death that ever happened, or is happening today, or will happen in the future behaves according to this one rule of existence.

To be sure, new forms do emerge with the passage of time, but they still conform to the same old principle.

How do I know that Tao is universal?

I cannot answer that rationally. I know it from being silent. I know it by virtue of God.

22. The Paradox of Letting Go

When I let go of what I am, I become what I might be. When I let go of what I have, I receive what I need.

These are feminine or *Yin* paradoxes:

- By yielding, I endure.
- The empty space is filled.
- When I give of myself, I become more.
- When I feel most destroyed, I am about to grow.
- When I desire nothing, a great deal comes to me.

Have you ever struggled to get work or love and finally given up and found both love and work were suddenly there?

Do you want to be free and independent? Conform to God's law; that is how everything happens anyway.

When I give up trying to impress the group, I become very impressive. But when I am just trying to make myself look good, the group knows that and does not like it.

My best work is done when I forget my own point of view; the less I make of myself, the more I am.

When I yield to the wishes of the person working, I encounter no resistance.

This is the wisdom of the feminine: let go in order to achieve. The wise leader demonstrates this.

23. Be Still

The wise leader speaks rarely and briefly. After all, no other natural outpouring goes on and on. It rains and then it stops. It thunders and then it stops.

The leader teaches more through being than through doing. The quality of one's silence conveys more than long speeches.

Be still. Follow your inner wisdom. In order to know your inner wisdom, you have to be still.

The leader who knows how to be still and feel deeply will probably be effective. But the leader who chatters and boasts and tries to impress the group has no center and carries little weight.

Tao works for those who follow Tao. God serves those who serve God. When you are in touch with the single principle, you can consciously cooperate with it.

If you consciously cooperate with the single principle, your actions will be effective. But if you are simply being egocentric, or if you are just trying to be dramatic, you will neither do good nor look good.

Remember that the method is awareness-of-process. Reflect. Be still.

What do you deeply feel?

24. Take It Easy

Trying too hard produces unexpected results:
- The flashy leader lacks stability.
- Trying to rush matters gets you nowhere.
- Trying to appear brilliant is not enlightened.
- Insecure leaders try to promote themselves.
- Impotent leaders capitalize on their position.
- It is not very holy to point out how holy you are.

All these behaviors come from insecurity. They feed insecurity. None of them helps the work. None contributes to the leader's health.

The leader who knows how things happen does not do these things.

Consider:

When you think that you are so good, what are you comparing yourself with? God? Or your own insecurities?

Do you want fame? Fame will complicate your life and compromise simplicity in your comings and goings.

Is it money? The effort of trying to get rich will steal your time.

Any form of egocentricity, of selfishness, obscures your deeper self and blinds you to how things happen.

25. Tao: Is and Isn't

This is what Tao is not:

- It is not a thing.
- It is not a sound or any other vibration.
- It is not divisible into parts.
- It does not change.
- It cannot be diluted or augmented.
- It has no partner or complement.

This is what Tao is:

- It is one; it is unity.
- It determines everything.
- It comes before everything.
- It is the law of everything.

The clearest, most helpful word I know to use for Tao is *How*, because Tao is the principle of how everything works.

Remember that while it has no form or qualities, it is everywhere, all the time, forever.

Imagine four levels of infinity: people are infinite in a sense; the earth is infinite; the cosmos is infinite; Tao is infinite. Although each of these four may be infinite in a way, the first three are subject to the next greater one.

People are dependent on the earth. The earth is dependent on the cosmos. The cosmos is dependent on Tao.

But Tao is not dependent on anything.

26. Center and Ground

The leader who is centered and grounded can work with erratic people and critical group situations without harm.

Being centered means having the ability to recover one's balance, even in the midst of action. A centered person is not subject to passing whims or sudden excitements.

Being grounded means being down-to-earth, having gravity or weight. I know where I stand, and I know what I stand for: that is ground.

The centered and grounded leader has stability and a sense of self.

One who is not stable can easily get carried away by the intensity of leadership and make mistakes of judgment or even become ill.

27. Beyond Techniques

An experienced traveler does not need a packaged tour to go places safely.

A good political speech does not need to make promises or antagonize the crowd.

A good mathematician does not need a computer to solve every problem.

A secure home does not have bolts and bars and locks and alarms everywhere, yet a burglar cannot get inside.

The wise leader's ability does not rest on techniques or gimmicks or set exercises. The method of awareness-of-process applies to all people and all situations.

The leader's personal state of consciousness creates a climate of openness. Center and ground give the leader stability, flexibility, and endurance.

Because the leader sees clearly, the leader can shed light on others.

The group members need the leader for guidance and facilitation. The leader needs people to work with, people to serve. If both do not recognize the mutual need to love and respect one another, each misses the point.

They miss the creativity of the student-teacher polarity. They do not see how things happen.

53

28. A Warrior, a Healer, and Tao

The leader can act as a warrior or as a healer.

As a warrior, the leader acts with power and decision. That is the *Yang* or masculine aspect of leadership.

Most of the time, however, the leader acts as a healer and is in an open, receptive, and nourishing state. That is the feminine or *Yin* aspect of leadership.

This mixture of doing and being, of warrior and healer, is both productive and potent.

There is a third aspect of leadership: Tao. Periodically, the leader withdraws from the group and returns to silence, returns to God.

Being, doing, being. . . then, Tao. I withdraw in order to empty myself of what has happened, to replenish my spirit.

A brilliant warrior does not make every possible brilliant intervention. A knowing healer takes time to nourish self as well as others.

Such simplicity and economy is a valuable lesson. It deeply affects the group.

The leader who knows when to listen, when to act, and when to withdraw can work effectively with nearly anyone, even with other professionals, group leaders, or therapists, perhaps the most difficult and sophisticated group members.

Because the leader is clear, the work is delicate and does not violate anybody's sensibilities.

29. The Paradox of Pushing

Too much force will backfire. Constant interventions and instigations will not make a good group. They will spoil a group.

The best group process is delicate. It cannot be pushed around. It cannot be argued over or won in a fight.

The leader who tries to control the group through force does not understand group process. Force will cost you the support of the members.

Leaders who push think that they are facilitating process, when in fact they are blocking process.

They think that they are building a good group field, when in fact they are destroying its coherence and creating factions.

They think that their constant interventions are a measure of ability, when in fact such interventions are crude and inappropriate.

They think that their leadership position gives them absolute authority, when in fact their behavior diminishes respect.

The wise leader stays centered and grounded and uses the least force required to act effectively. The leader avoids egocentricity and emphasizes being rather than doing.

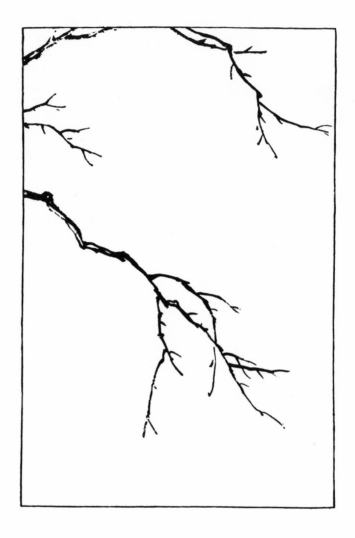

30. Force and Conflict

The leader who understands how process unfolds uses as little force as possible and runs the group without pressuring people.

When force is used, conflict and argument follow. The group field degenerates. The climate is hostile, neither open nor nourishing.

The wise leader runs the group without fighting to have things a certain way. The leader's touch is light. The leader neither defends nor attacks.

Remember that consciousness, not selfishness, is both the means of teaching and the teaching itself.

Group members will challenge the ego of one who leads egocentrically. But one who leads selflessly and harmoniously will grow and endure.

31. Harsh Interventions

There are times when it seems as if one must intervene powerfully, suddenly, and even harshly. The wise leader does this only when all else fails.

As a rule, the leader feels more wholesome when the group process is flowing freely and unfolding naturally, when delicate facilitations far outnumber harsh interventions.

Harsh interventions are a warning that the leader may be uncentered or have an emotional attachment to whatever is happening. A special awareness is called for.

Even if harsh interventions succeed brilliantly, there is no cause for celebration. There has been injury. Someone's process has been violated.

Later on, the person whose process has been violated may well become less open and more defended. There will be a deeper resistance and possibly even resentment.

Making people do what you think they ought to do does not lead toward clarity and consciousness. While they may do what you tell them to do at the time, they will cringe inwardly, grow confused, and plot revenge.

That is why your victory is actually a failure.

32. Unity

Tao cannot be defined. One can only say that it is the single principle responsible for every event or thing.

When the leader has regard for this principle, and for no lesser theories, the group members trust the leader. Because the leader pays equal attention to everything that happens, there are no prejudices to divide the group into factions. There is unity.

Because the group work is grounded in an obvious and natural righteousness, rules and regulations are not needed to make people behave.

Even though the single principle cannot be defined, it is possible to explain what is happening in a group. We speak of gestalt formation, of polarities, of flows and blocks, of interventions that either hinder or facilitate, and so on.

But too much theoretical talk distracts the group from what is happening, from the process itself. Talking about process is one way to block process and lower the energy of the group field.

When that happens, the wise leader returns once again to an awareness of what is happening and to the single principle that lies behind what is happening.

In the long run, focusing on this single principle is the most potent aspect of leadership. From this unity, we learn how things happen.

33. Inner Resources

To know how other people behave takes intelligence, but to know myself takes wisdom.

To manage other people's lives takes strength, but to manage my own life takes true power.

If I am content with what I have, I can live simply and enjoy both prosperity and free time.

If my goals are clear, I can achieve them without fuss.

If I am at peace with myself, I will not spend my life force in conflicts.

If I have learned to let go, I do not need to fear dying.

34. All Inclusive

The single principle can be found everywhere, all the time. Everything works according to it. Every life unfolds according to it. The single principle does not say yes to this and no to that.

Even though Tao is the source of all growth and development, nothing profits Tao. Tao benefits all without return and without prejudice.

Neither is the single principle private property. You cannot own it. It does not own you.

Its greatness lies in its universality. It is all-inclusive.

The wise leader follows this principle and does not act selfishly. The leader does not accept one person and refuse to work with another. The leader does not own people or control their lives. Leadership is not a matter of winning.

The work is done in order to shed the light of awareness on whatever is happening: also, selfless service, without prejudice, available to all.

35. Keep It Simple

Do not get carried away by the group process.

Stick to the single principle. Then you can do good work, stay free from chaos and conflicts, and feel present in all situations.

The superficial leader cannot see how things happen, even though the evidence is everywhere. This leader is swept up by drama, sensation, and excitement. All this confusion is blinding.

But the leader who returns again and again to awareness-of-process has a deep sense of how things happen. This leader has a simple time of it. The sessions flow smoothly, and when the group ends, the leader is still in good spirits.

36. Polarities, Paradoxes, and Puzzles

All behaviors contain their opposites:

- Hyper-inflation leads to collapse.
- A show of strength suggests insecurity.
- What goes up must come down.
- If you want to prosper, be generous.

Also:

- The feminine outlasts the masculine.
- The feminine allows, but the masculine causes.
- The feminine surrenders, then encompasses and wins.

And:

- Water wears away the rock.
- Spirit overcomes force.
- The weak will undo the mighty.

Learn to see things backwards, inside out, and upside down.

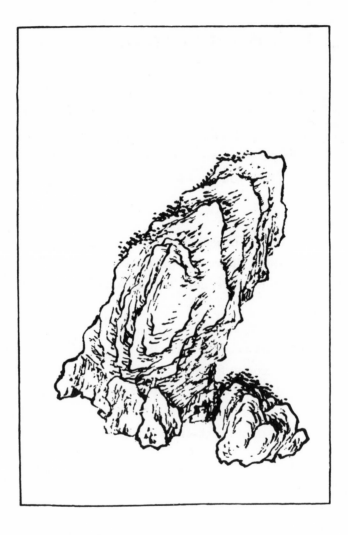

37. Doing Little

It puzzles people at first, to see how little the able leader actually does, and yet how much gets done.

But the leader knows that is how things work. After all, Tao does nothing at all, yet everything gets done.

When the leader gets too busy, the time has come to return to selfless silence.

Selflessness gives one center.

Center creates order.

When there is order, there is little to do.

38. Potent Leadership

Potent leadership is a matter of being aware of what is happening in the group and acting accordingly. Specific actions are less important than the leader's clarity or consciousness. That is why there are no exercises or formulas to ensure successful leadership.

Potency cannot be calculated or manipulated, nor is it a matter of trying to look good.

Three examples illustrate differing degrees of potency in leadership:

1. Potent: a conscious yet spontaneous response to what is happening in the here-and-now; no calculation or manipulation.

2. Less Potent: trying to do what is right. This is calculated behavior based on a concept of right, and manipulative behavior based on an idea of what should happen.

3. Least Potent: imposed morality. Imposed morality rests entirely on should and shouldn't. It is both calculated and manipulative, and meets resistance with punishment. It sheds no light on what is actually happening. It often backfires.

Leaders who lose touch with what is happening cannot act spontaneously, so they try to do what they think is right. If that fails, they often try coercion.

But the wise leader who loses the sense of immediacy becomes quiet and lets all effort go until a sense of clarity and consciousness returns.

39. The Source of Power

Natural events are potent because they act in accordance with how things work. They simply are.

Study natural processes: the light in the sky, the gravity of earth, the unfolding of your own ideas and insights, the emptiness of space, the fullness of life, and the behavior of saints.

Imagine what would happen if these processes were neurotic and self-centered: a lazy sky flickers; gravity varies from moment to moment; your mind is irrational; space is agitated; life is abortive; the saints are worthless models. Nothing works.

The wise leader knows better than to be neurotic and self-centered. Potency comes from knowing what is happening and acting accordingly. Paradoxically, freedom comes from obedience to the natural order.

Since all creation is a whole, separateness is an illusion. Like it or not, we are team players. Power comes through cooperation, independence through service, and a greater self through selflessness.

40. Meditate

Learn to return to your self.

Become silent: What is happening when nothing is happening?

Can you tell the difference between what is happening and how it happens?

Can you sense how what is happening arises out of how it happens?

Process. . . and principle.

41. Disturbing Wisdom

The wise leader, learning how things happen, lives accordingly.

The average leader also learns how things happen, but vacillates, now acting accordingly and then forgetting.

The worst leaders learn how things happen and dismiss the single principle as total nonsense. How else could their work be so futile?

After all, they say, any principle that does not get you love or money or power must be useless. A silent mind is a dumb mind. Selflessness is no way to get ahead. Virtue is for fools. Kindness is weakness. And so on.

This is a problem: because the wise leader's only allegiance is to how things happen, people who do not see how things happen naturally think that the wise leader's behavior has no basis in reality. Also, the leader's silence and manner of being are disturbing. Because the leader's motives are obscure, the leader is hard to figure out.

The problem comes back to the fact that the principle is not a thing and cannot be defined. That does not make sense to some people.

It is not easy to understand a person whose foundation is invisible.

Creative Process

The principle is not a thing. Call it *zero*.

The principle in action is the unity of creation. This unity is a single whole. Call it *one*.

Creation consists of pairs of opposites or polarities. Call these polarities or pairs *two*'s.

These polarities become creative when they interact. Their interaction is the third element. Call it *three*.

For example, a man and a woman are two. Their interaction, or intercourse, the third element, makes babies. That is creative. That is how all creativity occurs.

The wise leader knows about pairs of opposites and their interactions. The leader knows how to be creative.

In order to lead, the leader learns how to follow. In order to prosper, the leader learns to live simply. In both cases, it is the interaction that is creative.

Leading without following is sterile. Trying to become rich by accumulating more and more is a full-time career and not free at all.

Being one-sided always produces unexpected and paradoxical results. Being well-defended will not protect you; it will diminish your life and eventually kill you.

Exceptions to these examples of traditional wisdom are very hard to find.

43. Gentle Interventions

entle interventions, if they are clear, overcome rigid resistances.

If gentleness fails, try yielding or stepping back altogether. When the leader yields, resistances relax.

Generally speaking, the leader's consciousness sheds more light on what is happening than any number of interventions or explanations.

Few leaders realize how much how little will do.

44. Owning or Being Owned?

Are you doing this work to facilitate growth or to become famous?

Which is more important: acquiring more possessions or becoming more conscious?

Which works better: getting or letting go?

There is a problem with owning a lot. There is a problem with getting more and more.

The more you have and the more you get, the more you have to look after. The more you might lose. Is that owning or being owned?

But if you give up things, you can give up spending your life looking after things.

Try being still in order to discover your inner security. If you have inner security, you will have what you want anyway. Also you will be less harried, and you will last longer.

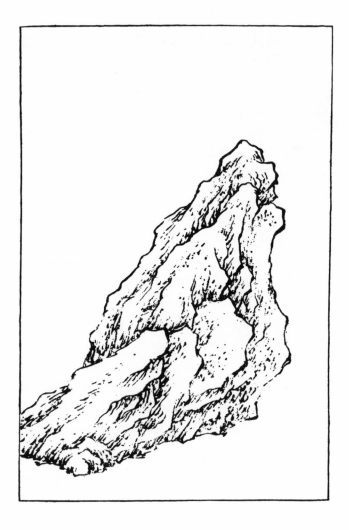

45. Appearing Foolish

The best work often seems idiotically simple to group members who are unaccustomed to this sort of leadership. Yet a great deal happens.

Perhaps it looks as if the leader is only sitting there and has no idea of what to do. But it is just this lack of needless intervention that permits the group to grow and be fertile.

Perhaps some disappointed group member expected an expert who would expound freely. But what this leader says is so obvious, it often sounds simple-minded. Even this leader's honesty seems strangely perplexing.

Appearing foolish does not matter. When you are cold, you flap your arms about to get warm. But when you are overheated, you keep still. That is common sense.

The leader's stillness overcomes the group's agitation. The leader's consciousness is the primary tool of this work.

46. Nothing to Win

The well-run group is not a battlefield of egos. Of course there will be conflict, but these energies become creative forces.

If the leader loses sight of how things happen, quarrels and fear devastate the group field.

This is a matter of attitude. There is nothing to win or lose in group work. Making a point does not shed light on what is happening. Wanting to be right blinds people.

The wise leader knows that it is far more important to be content with what is actually happening than to get upset over what might be happening but isn't.

47. Here and Now

The wise leader knows what is happening in a group by being aware of what is happening here and now. This is more potent than wandering off into various theories or making complex interpretations of the situation at hand.

Stillness, clarity, and consciousness are more immediate than any number of expeditions into the distant lands of one's mind.

Such expeditions, however stimulating, distract both the leader and the group members from what is actually happening.

By staying present and aware of what is happening, the leader can do less yet achieve more.

48. Unclutter Your Mind

Beginners acquire new theories and techniques until their minds are cluttered with options.

Advanced students forget their many options. They allow the theories and techniques that they have learned to recede into the background.

Learn to unclutter your mind. Learn to simplify your work.

As you rely less and less on knowing just what to do, your work will become more direct and more powerful. You will discover that the quality of your consciousness is more potent than any technique or theory or interpretation.

Learn how fruitful the blocked group or individual suddenly becomes when you give up trying to do just the right thing.

49. Be Open to Whatever Emerges

The wise leader does not impose a personal agenda or value system on the group.

The leader follows the group's lead and is open to whatever emerges. The leader judges no one and is attentive to both 'good' and 'bad' people. It does not even matter whether a person is telling the truth or lying.

Being open and attentive is more effective than being judgmental. This is because people naturally tend to be good and truthful when they are being received in a good and truthful manner.

Perhaps the leader seems naive and childlike in this uncritical openness to whatever emerges. But openness is simply more potent than any system of judgments ever devised.

50. Existence: Life and Death

Existence consists of both life and death. Favoring either life or death denies existence and creates tension. Tension causes people to make mistakes in critical situations. Mistakes are far more deadly than existence itself.

Thirty percent of the people love life and fear death.
Another thirty percent prefer death and avoid life.
Another thirty percent fear both life and death.

Ninety percent of the people suffer the tension that comes from ignorance of how polarities work. Even though life and death are opposites, they are inseparable. Preferences are futile.

Only ten percent have the wisdom to accept both life and death as facts and simply enjoy the dance of existence. After all, growth and decay are everywhere, all the time.

The wise leader knows that everything comes and goes. So why grasp or cling? Why worry or cringe? Why live in a fantasy of what might happen?

The ferocious dog bites the excited person. The conscious and centered person walks by unharmed.

The wise leader exists without either loving death or fearing death. This freedom keeps the leader safe from harm.

51. Principle and Process

verything, every behavior, is a vibratory pattern or process. Such process emerges, develops, and decays, according to the single principle.

People have a natural reverence for the principle, and they naturally love the vibratory energy which obeys the principle.

The vibratory energy and the principle make a partnership, which produces an infinite variety of forms. But the partnership takes no profit from its productivity. Neither does it get its power by making things happen in a coercive manner. There are simply no alternatives; there is no other way.

This partnership between principle and process is the first fact of life and of our work.

52. The Womb

All creation consists of polarities. The fundamental polarity of creation is called Plus/Minus, *Yin/Yang*, or Feminine/Masculine.

This fundamental polarity is self-impregnating. It is an androgynous womb which produces everything.

Everything includes me. I am a process consisting of polarities, which develop according to the single principle. I am a child of God. I come from the womb of creation.

This knowledge gives me stability.

If I were to put my faith in some thing or person or creed, I would have no stability. People and things and creeds come and go and change all the time. I would live in fear that the thing I adored would be lost, or the person I obeyed would die, or the creed I followed would be altered.

So my only allegiance is to the single principle.

I can look at a person and see both principle and process in them. I can see how they work. I can see them actually working. That is the basis of my ability as a group leader.

From knowing how things work, I also know the importance of staying flexible. Everything that grows is flexible. All enduring strength is flexible.

I know too that my allegiance to principle and process means that I am not afraid of dying. I have nothing to lose. I know that I am an aspect of the Eternal. My home is the womb of creation. Dying is going home.

53. Materialism

The wise leader leads a quiet and meditative life. But most people are busy getting as many possessions as they can.

The quiet path leads toward a more conscious existence. The busy path creates an exaggerated materialism.

Becoming more conscious leads toward God and a sense of the unity of all creation. But excessive consumption is only possible by exploiting someone.

The world's goods are unevenly distributed. Some have a great deal. Most have very little. We are running out of enough resources to go around. Everyone knows that.

Yet those who are already encumbered by possessions get more and more. They even brag about how much they have. Don't they know what stealing is?

Owning lots of possessions does not come from God. People get it by manipulating other people.

54. The Ripple Effect

Do you want to be a positive influence in the world? First, get your own life in order. Ground yourself in the single principle so that your behavior is wholesome and effective. If you do that, you will earn respect and be a powerful influence.

Your behavior influences others through a ripple effect. A ripple effect works because everyone influences everyone else. Powerful people are powerful influences.

If your life works, you influence your family.

If your family works, your family influences the community.

If your community works, your community influences the nation.

If your nation works, your nation influences the world.

If your world works, the ripple effect spreads throughout the cosmos.

Remember that your influence begins with you and ripples outward. So be sure that your influence is both potent and wholesome.

How do I know that this works?

All growth spreads outward from a fertile and potent nucleus. You are a nucleus.

55. Vital Energy

People who surrender all their blocks and conflicts experience a free flow of vital energy.

They look as radiant as a baby, and they enjoy a child-like immunity to injury. Bugs won't bite them. Dogs don't attack them. Trouble-makers leave them alone.

Their bodies seem relaxed and pliant, but their stamina and strength are remarkable. They are sexually moving without being overtly erotic. They can sing or even yell for a long time and never get hoarse.

It is as if they were newly in love, not with one person, but with all creation, and their energies are as abundant as all creation.

It is a mistake to confuse excitement or arousal with the vital flow of enlightenment. Stimulants and emotional adventures arouse people, but such arousal does not enhance one's energies. On the contrary, excitement spends energy and exhausts vitality.

Think of excitement as tension that comes when stimulation meets resistance. The exciting experience ends when the stimulation stops or when a person wears out.

But the vitality of enlightenment is a continuous flow. It meets no resistance and goes on and on without stress.

Excitement is rooted in passing desires. Vital energy springs from the eternal.

56. The Leader's Integrity

The wise leader knows that the true nature of events cannot be captured in words. So why pretend?

Confusing jargon is one sure sign of a leader who does not know how things happen.

But what cannot be said can be demonstrated: be silent, be conscious. Consciousness works. It sheds light on what is happening. It clarifies conflicts and harmonizes the agitated individual or group field.

The leader also knows that all existence is a single whole. Therefore, the leader is a neutral observer who takes no sides.

The leader cannot be seduced by offers or threats. Money, love, or fame—whether gained or lost—do not sway the leader from center.

The leader's integrity is not idealistic. It rests on a pragmatic knowledge of how things work.

57. Doing Less and Being More

Run an honest, open group.

Your job is to facilitate and illuminate what is happening. Interfere as little as possible. Interference, however brilliant, creates a dependency on the leader.

The fewer rules the better. Rules reduce freedom and responsibility. Enforcement of rules is coercive and manipulative, which diminishes spontaneity and absorbs group energy.

The more coercive you are, the more resistant the group will become. Your manipulations will only breed evasions. Every law creates an outlaw. This is no way to run a group.

The wise leader establishes a clear and wholesome climate in the group room. In the light of awareness, the group naturally acts in a wholesome manner.

When the leader practices silence, the group remains focused. When the leader does not impose rules, the group discovers its own goodness. When the leader acts unselfishly, the group simply does what is to be done.

Good leadership consists of doing less and being more.

58. Unfolding Process

Group process evolves naturally. It is self-regulating. Do not interfere. It will work itself out.

Efforts to control process usually fail. Either they block process or make it chaotic.

Learn to trust what is happening. If there is silence, let it grow; something will emerge. If there is a storm, let it rage; it will resolve into calm.

Is the group discontented? You can't make it happy. Even if you could, your efforts might well deprive the group of a very creative struggle.

The wise leader knows how to facilitate the unfolding group process, because the leader is also a process. The group's process and the leader's process unfold in the same way, according to the same principle.

The leader knows how to have a profound influence without making things happen.

For example, facilitating what is happening is more potent than pushing for what you wish were happening. Demonstrating or modeling behaviors is more potent than imposing morality. Unbiased positions are stronger than prejudice. Radiance encourages people, but outshining everyone else inhibits them.

59. The Source of Your Ability

Whether you are leading a group or going about your daily life, you need to be conscious. You need to be aware of what is happening and how things happen. If you are aware of what is happening and how things happen, you can act accordingly. You can steer clear of trouble, and be both vital and effective.

Remember that you too are a natural process. Being aware of how things happen includes being aware of yourself. Your life unfolds according to the same principle that governs every other unfolding. You are rooted in the common ground of all creation.

Being like everything else means that you are ordinary. But consciously knowing that you are like everything else is extraordinary. And knowing how that universality works and having the sense to act accordingly is the source of your power, your endurance, and your excellence.

Consciousness or awareness, then, is the source of your ability. Learn to become increasingly conscious.

60. Don't Stir Things Up

Run the group delicately, as if you were cooking small fish.

As much as possible, allow the group process to emerge naturally. Resist any temptation to instigate issues or elicit emotions which have not appeared on their own.

If you stir things up, you will release forces before their time and under unwarranted pressure. They may be emotions that belong to other people or places. They may be unspecific or chaotic energies which, in response to your pressure, strike out and hit any available target.

These forces are real and exist within the group. But do not push. Allow them to come out when they are ready.

When hidden issues and emotions emerge naturally, they resolve themselves naturally. They are not harmful. In fact, they are no different from any other thoughts or feelings.

All energies naturally arise, take form, grow strong, come to a new resolution, and finally pass away.

61. The Lowly Receptacle

It is a mistake to believe that a great leader is above others. Paradoxically, greatness comes from knowing how to be lowly and empty and receptive and of service.

Imagine that the life force is like water in the river and in the sea. The sea, greater than the river, lies below, open and receptive. The busy, rushing river enters the sea, is absorbed, and is transformed.

Or imagine that the leader is the feminine, lying below and open, empty, and receptive. The group member is the masculine, above, tense, and full. The feminine receives the masculine and absorbs the masculine vibration. Soon the feminine has encompassed the masculine; the masculine has spent itself, become soft and resolved.

The wise leader is of service: receptive, yielding, following. The group member's vibration dominates and leads, while the leader follows. But soon it is the member's consciousness which is transformed, the member's vibration which is resolved.

The relationship is reciprocal. It is the job of the leader to be aware of the group member's process; it is the need of the group member to be received and paid attention to.

Both get what they need, if the leader has the wisdom to serve and follow, to be open and below.

62. Whether You Know It or Not

Aperson does not have to join a group or be a wise leader to work things out. Life's process unfolds naturally. Conflicts resolve themselves sooner or later, whether or not a person knows how things happen.

It is true that being aware of how things happen makes one's words more potent and one's behavior more effective.

But even without the light of consciousness, people grow and improve. Being unconscious is not a crime; it is merely a lack of a very helpful ability.

Knowing how things work gives the leader more real power and ability than all the degrees or titles the world can offer.

That is why people in every era and in every culture have honored those who know how things happen.

63. Encounters

The wise leader knows how to act effectively.

To act effectively, be aware and unbiased. If you are aware, you will know what is happening; you will not act rashly. If you are unbiased, you can react in a balanced and centered manner.

Have respect for every person and every issue directed at you. Do not dismiss any encounter as insignificant. But neither should you become anxious or afraid of being overwhelmed or embarrassed.

If you are attacked or criticized, react in a way that will shed light on the event. This is a matter of being centered and of knowing that an encounter is a dance and not a threat to your ego or existence. Tell the truth.

If you are conscious of what is happening in a group, you will recognize emerging situations long before they have gotten out of hand. Every situation, no matter how vast or complex it may become, begins both small and simple.

Neither avoid nor seek encounters, but be open and when an encounter arises, respond to it while it is still manageable. There is no virtue in delaying until heroic action is needed to set things right. In this way, potentially difficult situations become simple.

If you have not bragged about your abilities or tried to make people be the way you think they ought to be, very few group members will want to encounter you anyway.

64. The Beginning, the Middle, And the End

Learn to recognize beginnings. At birth, events are relatively easy to manage. Slight interventions shape and guide easily. Potential difficulties can be avoided. The greatest danger lies in disrupting the emerging process by using too much force.

The wise leader sees things almost before they happen. A tree that is stiff and rigid begins as a pliant sapling. A great construction project begins with one shovelful of earth. A journey of a thousand miles begins with a single step.

Once an event is fully energized and formed, stand back as much as possible. Needless interventions will only confuse or block what is happening. Especially, do not try to make an event conform to any predetermined plan or model.

Many leaders spoil the work just as it nears completion. They get eager. They get invested in certain outcomes. They become anxious and make mistakes. This is a time for care and consciousness. Don't do too much. Don't be too helpful. Don't worry about getting credit for having done something.

Because the wise leader has no expectations, no outcome can be called a failure. Paying attention, allowing a natural unfolding, and standing back most of the time, the leader sees the event arrive at a satisfactory conclusion.

65. Theory and Practice

The leader's teachers did not emphasize complex theories. They practiced and taught a way of life based on consciousness and wisdom.

People who see the world in terms of theories often have a very intricate view of what is happening. Clarity is difficult for them. They are very hard to work with.

If you teach a group by making complex explanations, you will confuse people. They will take notes and fill their minds with opinions.

But if you return again and again to an awareness of what is actually happening, you will both clarify and enlighten .

The ability to distinguish between theory and practice will save you much trouble.

Practice a way of life, and demonstrate conscious cooperation with the single principle. If you cooperate with Tao, you will experience the power of universal harmony.

66. Low and Open

Why is the ocean the greatest body of water? Because it lies below all the rivers and streams and is open to them all.

What we call leadership consists mainly of knowing how to follow. The wise leader stays in the background and facilitates other people's process. The greatest things the leader does go largely unnoticed. Because the leader does not push or shape or manipulate, there is no resentment or resistance.

Group members genuinely appreciate a leader who facilitates their lives rather than promoting some personal agenda. Because the leader is open, any issue can be raised. Because the leader has no position to defend and shows no favoritism, no one feels slighted; no one wishes to quarrel.

67. Three Leadership Qualities

Here is a paradox: even though the single principle of how everything happens is great, those who follow the principle know that they are ordinary.

Great egocentricity does not make a person great. The common ground of all creation is a greater source of life than any exalted isolation.

These three qualities are invaluable to the leader:

- Compassion for all creatures
- Material simplicity or frugality
- A sense of equality or modesty.

A compassionate person acts in behalf of everyone's right to life. Material simplicity gives one an abundance to share. A sense of equality is, paradoxically, one's true greatness.

It is a mistake to consider a person whose only interest is self-interest as either caring or courageous. It is a mistake to rationalize that excessive consumption contributes to the well-being of others by giving them employment. It is a mistake to imagine that a person who acts immodestly or in a superior way is, in fact, a genuinely superior person.

These are all egocentric behaviors. They isolate a person from the common ground of existence. They produce rigidity and death.

Compassion, sharing, and equality, on the other hand, sustain life. This is because we are all one. When I care for you, I enhance the harmonious energy of the whole. And that is life.

68. Opportunities

The greatest martial arts are the gentlest. They allow an attacker the opportunity to fall down.

The greatest generals do not rush into every battle. They offer the enemy many opportunities to make self-defeating errors.

The greatest administrators do not achieve production through constraints and limitations. They provide opportunities.

Good leadership consists of motivating people to their highest levels by offering them opportunities, not obligations.

That is how things happen naturally. Life is an opportunity and not an obligation.

69. A Fight

If a group member wants to fight with you, consider the strategy of the guerrilla commander:

Never seek a fight. If it comes to you, yield; step back. It is far better to step back than to overstep yourself.

Your strength is good intelligence: be aware of what is happening. Your weapon is not a weapon at all. It is the light of consciousness.

Advance only where you encounter no resistance. If you make a point, do not cling to it. If you win, be gracious.

The person who initiates the attack is off center and easily thrown. Even so, have respect for any attacker. Never surrender your compassion or use your skill to harm another needlessly.

In any event, the more conscious force will win.

70. This Is Nothing New

This way of living and leading groups is easy to understand. It is easy to do.

But not many leaders understand this approach. Very few use it in their work.

Frankly, it is too simple and ancient to attract much attention. As a rule, the greatest interest goes to the greatest novelty.

The wise leader, sticking to the single principle of how everything happens, does nothing new or original.

The wise leader appeals to a very few followers, to those who recognize that traditional wisdom is a treasure which often lies hidden beneath an ordinary appearance.

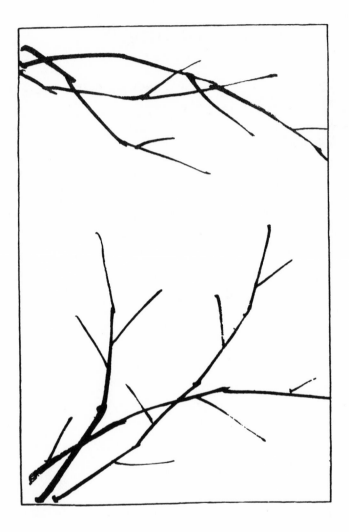

71. All the Answers

Nobody has all the answers. Knowing that you do not know everything is far wiser than thinking that you know a lot when you really don't.

Phony expertise is neurotic. Fortunately, once the symptoms are recognized, the cure is easy: stop it.

Probably every leader has tried this form of pretense at one time or another.

The wise leader has learned how painful it is to fake knowledge. Being wise and not wanting the pain, the leader does not indulge in pretending.

Anyway, it is a relief to be able to say: "I don't know."

72. Spiritual Awareness

Group work must include spiritual awareness if it is to touch the existential anxiety of our times. Without awe, the awful remains unspoken; a diffuse malaise remains.

Be willing to speak of traditional religion, no matter how offended some group members may be. Overcome the bias against the word God. The great force of our spiritual roots lies in tradition, like it or not.

The wise leader models spiritual behavior and lives in harmony with spiritual values. There is a way of knowing, higher than reason; there is a self, greater than egocentricity.

The leader demonstrates the power of selflessness and the unity of all creation.

73. Freedom and Responsibility

Imagine that there are two kinds of courage. One is an active courage that gets people killed. The other is an inner courage that keeps people alive.

Which of these two is better?

No one can answer that for you. Each has its benefits and its drawbacks. Tao has no preferences.

Keep in mind that Tao means how: how things happen. But how-things-happen is not the same as what-should-I-do. No one can tell you what to do. That is your freedom. That is your responsibility.

Instead of asking for advice, learn to become more conscious of what is actually happening. Then you will be able to see for yourself how things happen. You can make your own decisions about what to do.

Tao does not preach sermons or dictate behavior. What people do is their own responsibility. But the pattern of their behavior follows natural law.

This law is so general, it covers every possible event. It is so specific, it applies to every instance of every event.

But no one can decide for you what to do in a given situation. That is up to you.

74. Judge and Jury

It is not the leader's role to play judge and jury, to punish people for 'bad' behavior.

In the first place, punishment does not effectively control behavior.

But even if punishment did work, what leader would dare use fear as a teaching method?

The wise leader knows that there are natural consequences for every act. The task is to shed light on these natural consequences, not to attack the behavior itself.

If the leader tries to take the place of nature and act as judge and jury, the best you can expect is a crude imitation of a very subtle process.

At the very least, the leader will discover that the instrument of justice cuts both ways. Punishing others is punishing work.

75. Without Greed

The group will not prosper if the leader grabs the lion's share of the credit for the good work that has been done.

The group will rebel and resist if the leader relies on strict controls in an effort to make things come out a certain way.

The group members will become deadened and unresponsive if the leader is critical and harsh.

The wise leader is not greedy, selfish, defensive, or demanding. That is why the leader can be trusted to allow any event to unfold naturally.

76. Flexible or Rigid?

At birth, a person is flexible and flowing.

At death, a person becomes rigid and blocked.

Consider the lives of plants and trees: during their time of greatest growth, they are relatively tender and pliant. But when they are full grown or begin to die, they become tough and brittle.

The tree which has grown up and become rigid is cut into lumber.

The rigid group leader may be able to lead repetitious and structured exercises but can't cope with lively group process.

Whatever is flexible and flowing will tend to grow. Whatever is rigid and blocked will atrophy and die.

77. Cycles

Natural events are cyclical, always changing from one extreme toward an opposite.

Imagine a bow and arrow. As the archer draws the bow, the two tips of the bow, which were far apart, come closer together; the narrow space between string and wood becomes wide; the bow string, which was at rest, becomes taut.

When the archer releases the arrow, once again the process reverses itself, as the tension relaxes.

That is the way of nature: to relax what is tense, to fill what is empty, to reduce what is overflowing.

But a society based on materialism and the conquest of nature works to overcome these cycles. If some is good, more must be better, and an absolute glut seems best. At the same time, those who have little get even less.

The wise leader follows the natural order of events and does not take the consumer society for a model.

By serving others and being generous, the leader knows abundance. By being selfless, the leader helps others realize themselves. By being a disinterested facilitator, unconcerned with praise or pay, the leader becomes potent and successful.

The leader's behavior works because it is based on an understanding of opposites and cycles.

Effective behavior only seems backwards.

78. Soft and Strong

Water is fluid, soft, and yielding. But water will wear away rock, which is rigid and cannot yield.

As a rule, whatever is fluid, soft, and yielding will overcome whatever is rigid and hard.

The wise leader knows that yielding overcomes resistances, and gentleness melts rigid defenses.

The leader does not fight the force of the group's energy, but flows and yields and absorbs and lets go. A leader must endure a great deal of abuse. If the leader were not like water, the leader would break. The ability to be soft makes the leader a leader.

This is another paradox: what is soft is strong.

79. Win or Lose

If you get into an argument with a group member, and it does not come out the way you wish it would, do not pretend to compromise while withholding your true feelings.

Yield your position gracefully. Return to facilitating what is happening.

It is not your business to be right or to win arguments. It is not your business to find the flaws in the other person's position. It is not your business to feel belittled if the other person wins.

It is your business to facilitate whatever is happening, win or lose.

Because we are all one, there are no sides to take. When all is said and done, the wise leader goes along with what is happening anyway.

80. A Simple Life

If you want to be free, learn to live simply.

Use what you have and be content where you are. Quit trying to solve your problems by moving to another place, by changing mates or careers.

Leave your car in the garage. If you have a gun, put it away. Sell that complex computer and go back to using pencil and paper. Rather than read every new book that comes along, reread the classics.

Eat food grown locally. Wear simple, durable clothing. Keep a small home, uncluttered and easy to clean. Keep an open calendar with periods of uncommitted time. Have a spiritual practice and let family customs grow.

Of course, the world is full of novelty and adventures. New opportunities come along every day.

So what?

81. The Reward

It is more important to tell the simple, blunt truth than it is to say things that sound good. The group is not a contest of eloquence.

It is more important to act in behalf of everyone than it is to win arguments. The group is not a debating society.

It is more important to react wisely to what is happening than it is to be able to explain everything in terms of certain theories. The group is not a final examination for a college course.

The wise leader is not collecting a string of successes. The leader is helping others to find their own success. There is plenty to go around. Sharing success with others is very successful.

The single principle behind all creation teaches us that true benefit blesses everyone and diminishes no one.

The wise leader knows that the reward for doing the work arises naturally out of the work.